KINGFISHER EXPLORER BOOKS

SPACECRAFT

Robin Kerrod

Illustrated by
Roger Full, Tom Brittain
and Mike Saunders

Edited by Jill Coleman

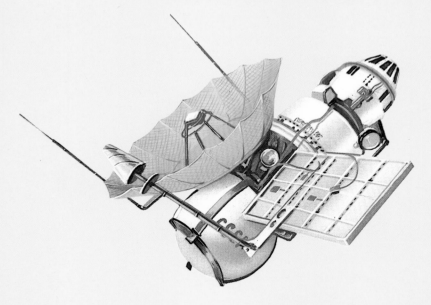

KINGFISHER BOOKS

Contents

About This Book

The first spacecraft, Sputnik 1, was launched into orbit by the USSR in 1957. Since then, spacecraft have carried people into orbit around the Earth and to the Moon. Unmanned spacecraft have explored the lunar surface and space probes have journeyed deep into space to examine and photograph the planets. Space stations, cruising in orbit for months, have provided unique conditions for scientific experiments. This book features the craft that pioneered space exploration, those in use now, and those of the future.

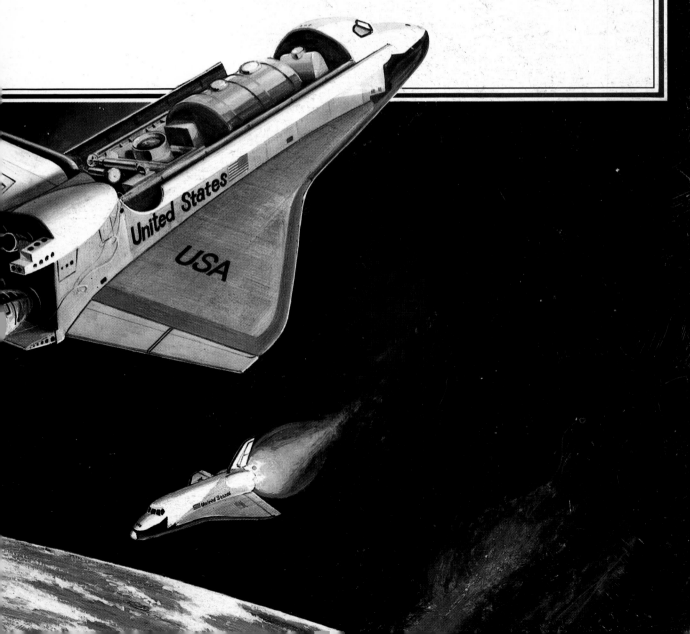

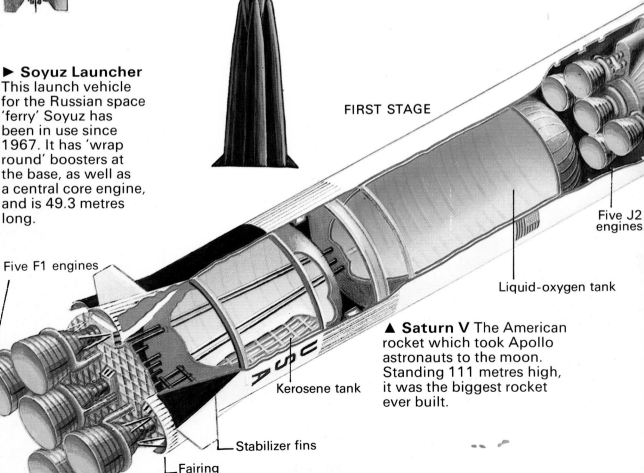

▼ **V2** Both the American and Russian space rockets are descendants of this World War II rocket bomb.

▶ **Soyuz Launcher** This launch vehicle for the Russian space 'ferry' Soyuz has been in use since 1967. It has 'wrap round' boosters at the base, as well as a central core engine, and is 49.3 metres long.

Launching Rockets

The rocket is the only kind of engine powerful enough to launch a spacecraft into orbit. It is also the only kind that will work in space, where there is no air. To do this, it burns a mixture of fuel and oxygen inside a chamber in the motor. The burning gases expand and rush out through the motor nozzle, thrusting the spacecraft forwards.

Space rockets use a vast amount of fuel to achieve the thrust necessary for space flight. The giant

FIRST STAGE

Five J2 engines

Liquid-oxygen tank

Five F1 engines

Kerosene tank

▲ **Saturn V** The American rocket which took Apollo astronauts to the moon. Standing 111 metres high, it was the biggest rocket ever built.

Stabilizer fins

Fairing

4

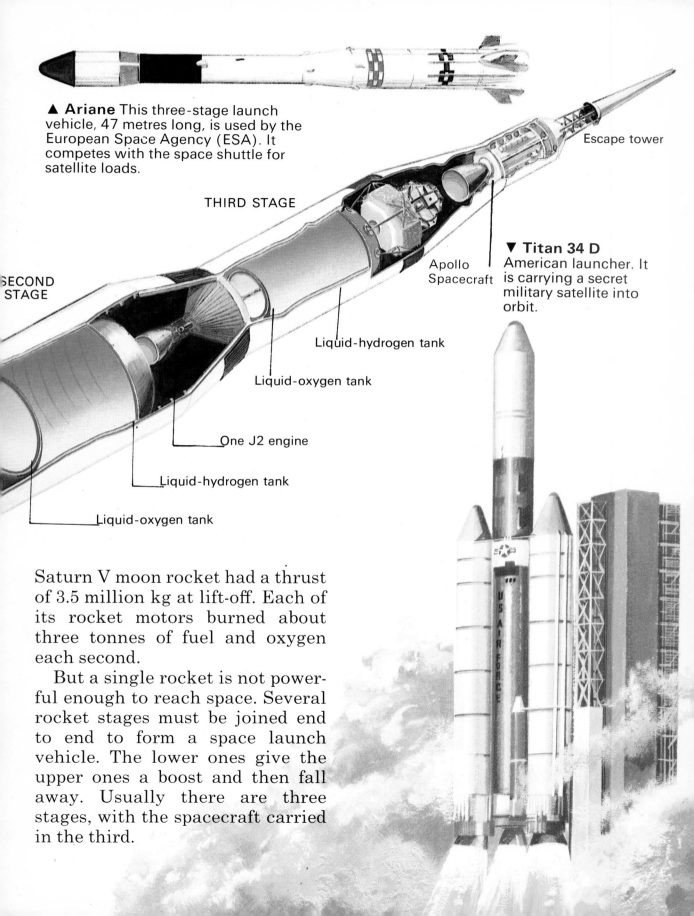

▲ Ariane This three-stage launch vehicle, 47 metres long, is used by the European Space Agency (ESA). It competes with the space shuttle for satellite loads.

THIRD STAGE

Escape tower

SECOND STAGE

Apollo Spacecraft

▼ Titan 34 D American launcher. It is carrying a secret military satellite into orbit.

Liquid-hydrogen tank

Liquid-oxygen tank

One J2 engine

Liquid-hydrogen tank

Liquid-oxygen tank

Saturn V moon rocket had a thrust of 3.5 million kg at lift-off. Each of its rocket motors burned about three tonnes of fuel and oxygen each second.

But a single rocket is not powerful enough to reach space. Several rocket stages must be joined end to end to form a space launch vehicle. The lower ones give the upper ones a boost and then fall away. Usually there are three stages, with the spacecraft carried in the third.

3.

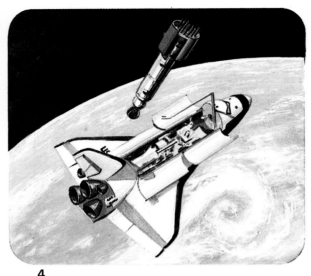

4.

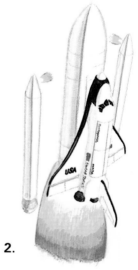

2.

1.

The Space Shuttle

A conventional launching vehicle can be used only once, which is wasteful and expensive. The United States has therefore developed the space shuttle, which is a reusable launch vehicle.

The main part of the shuttle is the orbiter, which carries the crew and cargo. Looking much like a delta-wing airliner, it is 37 metres long and has a wing space of 24 metres. The cavernous cargo bay of the orbiter is 18 metres long and 4.5 metres in diameter.

▶ **The shuttle orbiter** cut away to show the space laboratory Spacelab, which it can carry into space. Inside the pressurized module, teams of scientists and engineers will work for up to a month.

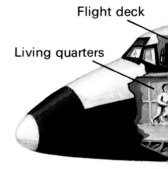

Flight deck

Living quarters

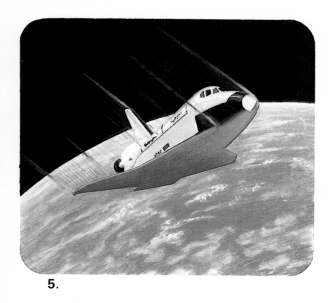

5.

6.

It is launched into space vertically like a rocket, astride a huge tank, which provides fuel for its three main liquid-propellant rocket engines. Strapped to the sides of the tank are two solid-propellant booster rockets, which fire at lift-off but then separate and parachute back to Earth to be re-used. The pictures show the operational sequence of the shuttle, ending with a runway landing.

1. Shuttle take-off. Side boosters and main engines fire together.
2. Their fuel used up, the boosters separate and parachute back to Earth.
3. Main tank separates.
4. Shuttle orbiter carries out operations in orbit.
5. After its mission the orbiter drops from orbit and re-enters the atmosphere.
6. With landing wheels down, the orbiter glides to a touchdown on the runway.

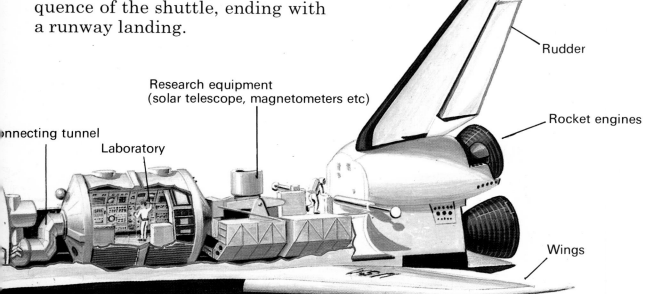

Rudder

Rocket engines

Wings

Research equipment
(solar telescope, magnetometers etc)

Connecting tunnel

Laboratory

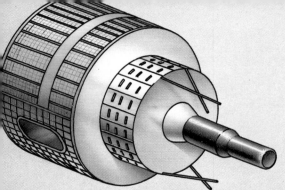

Man-Made Moons

◀ **Meteosat** is an advanced weather satellite developed by the European Space Agency.

▼ **Nimbus** One of the most successful American weather satellites since 1964. Its design was largely copied for the Landsat series of satellites.

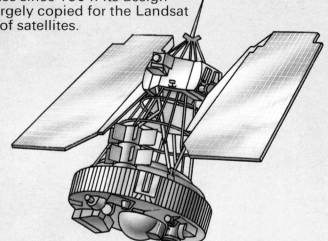

▶ **Molniya** This is one of Russia's communications satellites. It is part of a complex system which provides television, telephone and telegraph links to ground stations in Russia.

▼ **Space Telescope** When placed in orbit by the space shuttle, it will peer further into the depths of space than any Earth-based instruments.

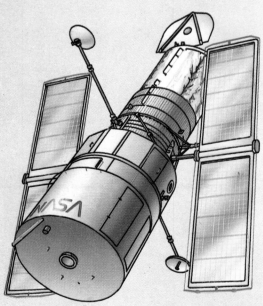

Every year, about a hundred artificial moons, or satellites, are launched into space. Some may remain there for centuries, others will be pulled down by the Earth's gravity after a few years. Most satellites carry solar cell panels, which turn the Sun's energy into electricity to power their instruments. These cells may cover the body of the satellite (as with Meteosat), or be arranged in separate 'wings' (as with Molniya).

Satellites have many different jobs to do. Weather satellites,

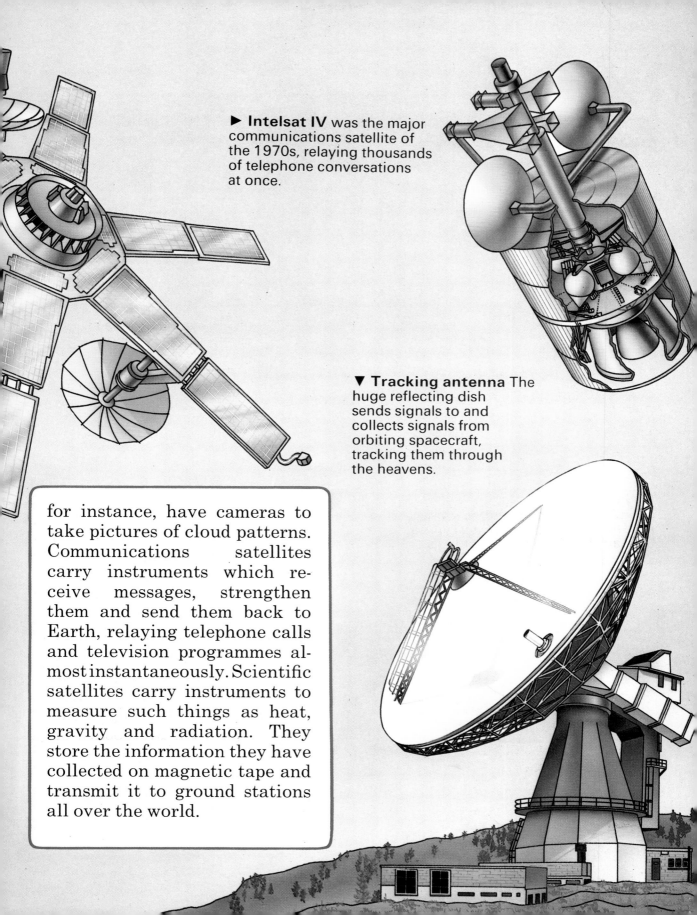

▶ **Intelsat IV** was the major communications satellite of the 1970s, relaying thousands of telephone conversations at once.

▼ **Tracking antenna** The huge reflecting dish sends signals to and collects signals from orbiting spacecraft, tracking them through the heavens.

for instance, have cameras to take pictures of cloud patterns. Communications satellites carry instruments which receive messages, strengthen them and send them back to Earth, relaying telephone calls and television programmes almost instantaneously. Scientific satellites carry instruments to measure such things as heat, gravity and radiation. They store the information they have collected on magnetic tape and transmit it to ground stations all over the world.

1.

2.

3.

Planetary Probes

Planetary probes are unmanned. They are launched in two stages. First they are rocketed into an Earth orbit and then the final stage of the rocket fires to head the craft towards a planet. After this the probe coasts for most of its journey without power. Unlike most satellites, planetary probes have small rocket engines, which are used occasionally as a brake, or to correct their flight path.

One of the first really successful probes was Mariner 4, which sent back close-up pictures of Mars in 1965. Later, American Viking probes released landing craft to look for signs of life on Mars. American Pioneer probes investigated Venus' thick atmosphere. Russian Venera probes have landed on the intensely hot surface and taken photographs.

American Pioneer and Voyager probes have flown by Jupiter, Saturn and Uranus, sending photographs back to Earth. In 1986, the European probe Giotto sent back pictures from the heart of Halley's Comet.

1. Viking spacecraft orbiting Mars.
2. Lander module separates from orbiter.
3. The parachute opens, the aeroshell is jettisoned and the lander's legs are extended.
4. Retro-rockets fire for a gentle touchdown.
5. Two Viking landers touched down in 1976. They found no convincing signs of Martian life.

Pioneer Venus

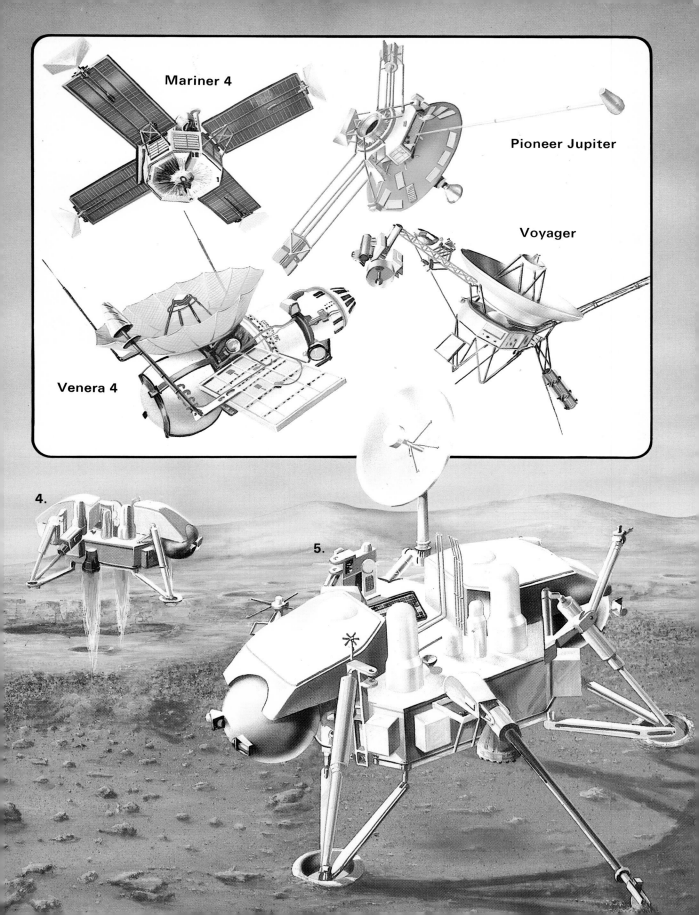

Mariner 4

Pioneer Jupiter

Voyager

Venera 4

4.

5.

Manned Spacecraft

A manned spacecraft has to be more complicated than an ordinary satellite. First, it must have a life-support system, to cope with the astronauts' bodily needs in space. Secondly, it must bring them safely back to Earth. Only part of it returns. This part is coated with a material that shields the returning astronauts from the fierce heat produced by friction as the craft plunges through the Earth's atmosphere.

Soyuz cosmonauts always land on the ground, firing retro-rockets beneath their craft to slow it down just before landing. Until the coming of the space shuttle, all American landings were made at sea.

▲ **Apollo** (1968–75) American three-man mooncraft, also used for Skylab visits and Apollo/Soyuz mission.

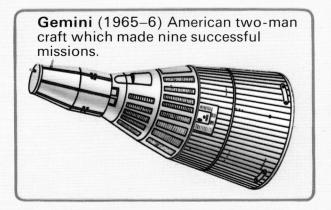

Gemini (1965–6) American two-man craft which made nine successful missions.

Mission Control

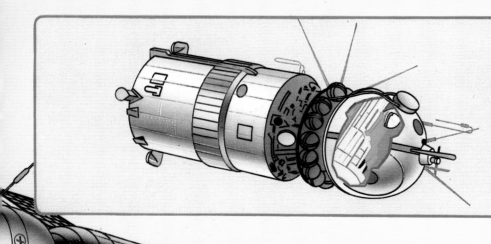

Vostok (1961–3) The Russian craft in which Yuri Gagarin made the first manned space flight on April 12 1961. Five more Vostok missions took place, one carrying the first woman in space.

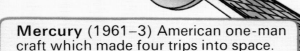

◄ **Soyuz** A Russian two-man craft, shown here, docked with an Apollo craft during the Apollo/Soyuz mission of 1975.

Mercury (1961–3) American one-man craft which made four trips into space.

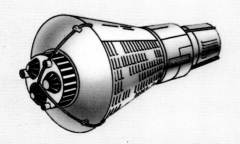

▼ **During a spacewalk** (called Extra Vehicular Activity or EVA) astronauts wear a helmeted spacesuit. Latest shuttle suits have a gas-propelled backpack. Unlike early astronauts (below) they are not linked to their craft by a lifeline.

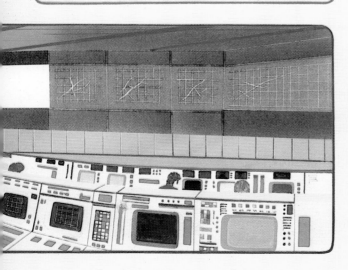

Lunar Explorers

Until the 1960s no-one knew what the Moon's surface was really like. Some people thought that it was firm and rocky; others feared that it was covered with dust too soft and thick for safe exploration. A series of lunar probes was launched to photograph possible landing sites and test the ground.

Though American probes eventually proved more successful, they were preceded by Russian ones. Russia's Luna 2 crash-landed on the Moon as early as 1959.

The American Ranger probes took pictures before crashing on the surface. Later, the Lunar Orbiters took photographs from orbit. The Surveyor probes actually soft-landed, proving that the surface of the Moon was suitable for manned landings.

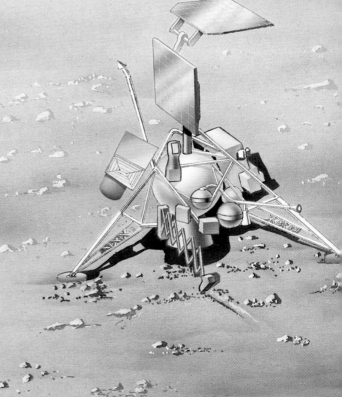

▼ **Surveyor** American soft-lander (1966–8). Later versions dug trenches in the lunar soil.

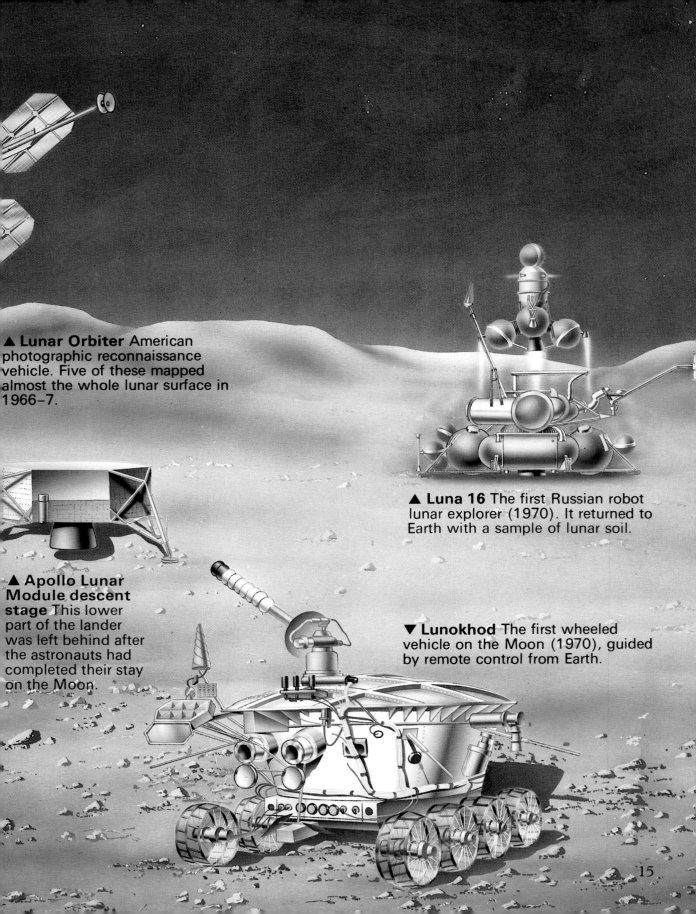

▲ **Lunar Orbiter** American photographic reconnaissance vehicle. Five of these mapped almost the whole lunar surface in 1966–7.

▲ **Apollo Lunar Module descent stage** This lower part of the lander was left behind after the astronauts had completed their stay on the Moon.

▲ **Luna 16** The first Russian robot lunar explorer (1970). It returned to Earth with a sample of lunar soil.

▼ **Lunokhod** The first wheeled vehicle on the Moon (1970), guided by remote control from Earth.

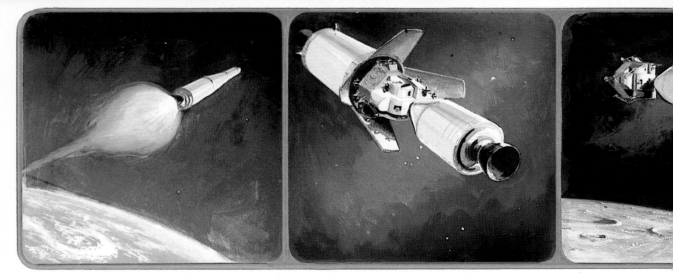

1.

2.

3.

Project Apollo

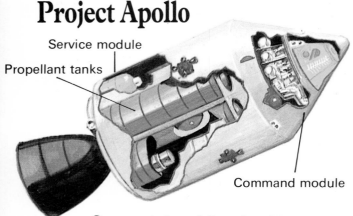

Service module

Propellant tanks

Command module

Command and Service Module (CSM) in which the three astronauts travelled to the Moon.

On 20 July 1969, three men set foot on the Moon. The spacecraft they travelled in was called Apollo. It was made up of three main parts: the command module (CM), together with the service module (SM) and the lunar module (LM). The pictures show the whole operation.

First, the Apollo spacecraft is launched into orbit (1), then the CSM and LM pull away from the launching rocket (2), blast off for the Moon and go into lunar

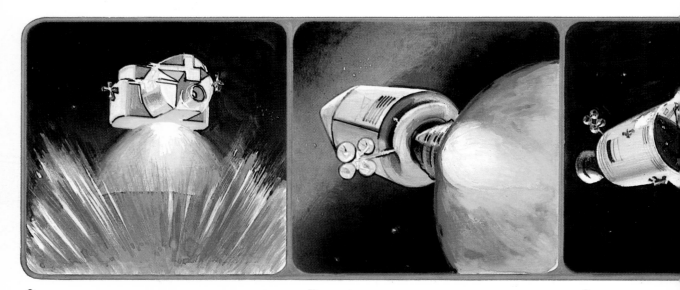

6.

7.

8.

4.

5.

orbit (3). The LM separates and swoops down on the Moon (4). Retro-firing, the LM makes a soft landing (5). After the Moon walk, the astronauts blast off from the Moon in the upper part of the LM (6). They transfer to the CSM and head for home (7). Before re-entry, the service module is discarded (8). The heat shield protects the men inside (9). Parachutes slow down the returning craft for a gentle splashdown (10).

Lunar Module (LM) in which astronauts Armstrong and Aldrin landed on the Moon.

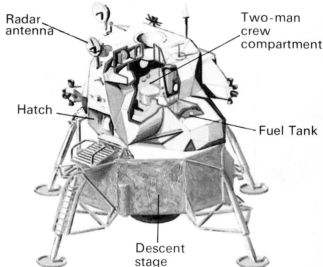

Radar antenna

Two-man crew compartment

Hatch

Fuel Tank

Descent stage

9.

10.

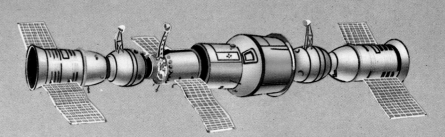

▲ **Salyut/Soyuz** Russia's successful prototype space station Salyut, with Soyuz ferries docked at each end.

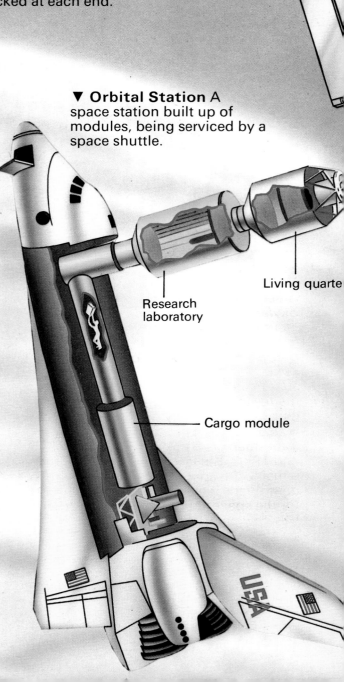

▼ **Orbital Station** A space station built up of modules, being serviced by a space shuttle.

Living quarte

Research laboratory

Cargo module

Space Stations

While the Americans concentrated on getting to the Moon, Russia set about establishing a permanent space station. The first station, Salyut, was launched in 1971. By the end of 1977 there were five more, the most successful being Salyut 6. Soyuz craft ferry visiting crews to and from the stations. Docking (linking) the two craft is a very skilled manoeuvre. In 1979 two Salyut cosmonauts smashed all records by spending 175 days in orbit.

The latest space station is Russia's Mir (meaning 'peace'). This permanently manned station has docking ports for up to six spacecraft.

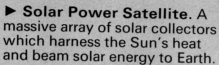

► **Solar Power Satellite.** A massive array of solar collectors which harness the Sun's heat and beam solar energy to Earth.

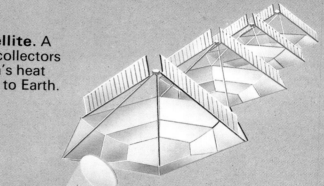

Research laboratory

Living quarters

Utility module

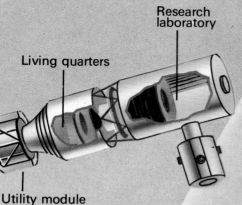

▼ **Industrial Module** A free-floating processing unit which provides special materials.

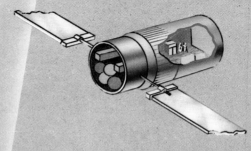

Skylab

The experimental American space station *Skylab* was built around an unused rocket stage left over from the *Apollo* programme. With *Apollo* docked to it, the space station measured 36 metres long and weighed over 90 tonnes. *Skylab* was occupied by three three-man crews in 1973 and 1974. The last crew remained in space for 84 days. Plans were made for the space shuttle to visit Skylab in 1980 to boost it into a higher orbit. But the space station fell out of the sky in July 1979, scattering fragments onto the Earth's surface.

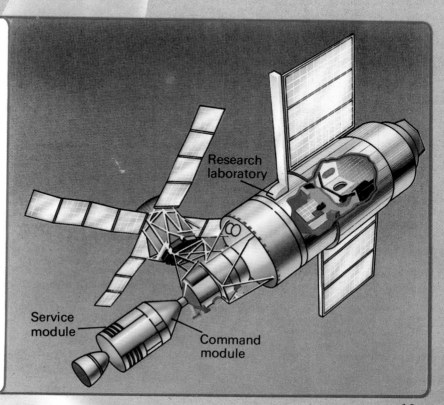

Research laboratory

Service module

Command module

Future Spacecraft

Many countries have now put spacecraft into orbit, including China, India and Japan. European countries, working together as the European Space Agency, have plans for future spacecraft. One idea is for a small two-person space shuttle called Hermes. ESA also has plans for fly-back boosters, with wings and small jet engines.

American plans include the mini-shuttle shown on the right. This would be taken into the air by a Boeing 747. Once in the stratosphere, the mini-shuttle would rocket into orbit.

Hermes on booster rocket

Re-usable fly-back booster

◄ **Hermes** is the name of Europe's mini-shuttle. If built, the craft would have room for a crew of two and a small cargo bay. The first-stage booster could fly back to the launch base.

▼ **Servicing vehicle** This craft is designed for orbital operations in the early 21st century. It would be controlled by a highly advanced robot computer system.

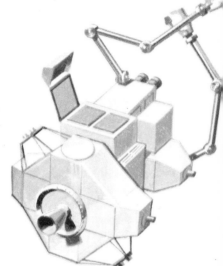

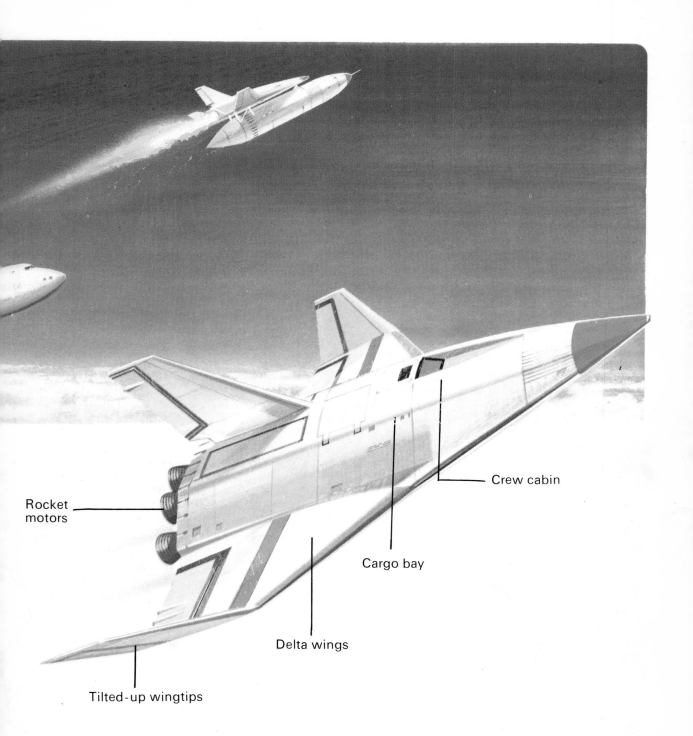

Rocket motors

Crew cabin

Cargo bay

Delta wings

Tilted-up wingtips

▲ **The mini-shuttle** is an 'instant-launch' concept for the 1990s. No launch base is necessary, just a runway long enough for the Boeing 747 carrier plane. After take-off and climb, a rocket motor mounted in the 747's tail boosts it higher and faster. The mini-shuttle then leaps off the plane's back, flying up into orbit using fuel from its underslung belly fuel tank. This would then be dropped. Craft like the mini-shuttle would be ideal for emergency rescues, fast placing of satellites in orbit, and for military spy missions.

Stepping Out

Outside the spacecraft, astronauts need to wear special clothing to protect them from the freezing cold and boiling Sun of space. Their suit also contains an oxygen supply and drinks unit.

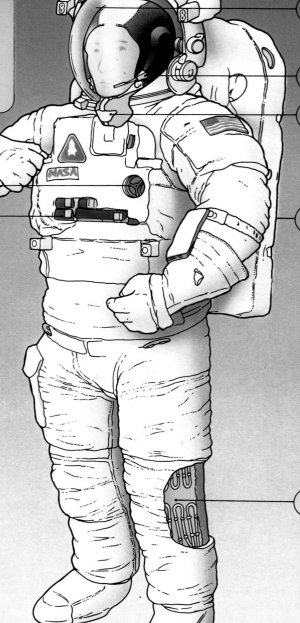

KEY
1 Pack containing TV camera and lights
2 Visor coated with thin layer of 'sunglass' gold
3 Microphone
4 Drinks unit
5 Backpack
6 Multi-layer suit and gloves
7 Oxygen controls
8 Heating controls
9 Cooling/ventilation garment
10 Boots

Glossary

Airlock An airtight cabin through which astronauts enter or leave a spacecraft.

Astronaut A person who travels in space.

Cosmonaut The Russian word for astronaut.

Docking The joining together of two spacecraft.

EVA Means Extra-Vehicular-Activity or space walking.

G-Forces The forces astronauts experience when their spacecraft suddenly accelerates or slows down.

Gravity A force by which bodies are attracted to each other.

Heat Shield A covering on the outside of a spacecraft which protects it from the heat of re-entry.

Module A part of a spacecraft.

NASA The American space agency; initials stand for National Aeronautics and Space Administration.

Orbit The path a spacecraft follows around the Earth, or around another body in space.

Payload The cargo of a spacecraft.

Probe A spacecraft sent to explore the Moon or the planets.

Re-entry The moment when a spacecraft re-enters the atmosphere after a space mission.

Retro-rocket A rocket that is fired against the direction of travel to act as a brake.

Satellite A body that circles a planet. The Moon is a natural satellite of the Earth. Spacecraft orbiting the Earth are artificial satellites.

Solar Cell A battery that changes the energy in sunlight into electricity.

Sputnik The Russian name for a satellite.

Step Rocket A 'piggy-back' arrangement of rockets used in space launchings.

Index

This revised expanded edition published in 1988 by
Kingfisher Books, Grisewood & Dempsey Ltd,
Elsley House, 24–30 Great Titchfield Street,
London W1P 7AD
Originally published in small format paperback
by Pan Books Ltd in 1980

Cover designed by David Jefferis
Cover and gatefold artwork by Janos Marphy/
  Jillian Burgess Agency

BRITISH LIBRARY CATALOGUING IN PUBLICATION DATA
  Spacecraft.—Rev.ed.—(Kingfisher
  explorer books).
  1. Space vehicles—Juvenile literature
  I. Title II. Kerrod, Robin. Guide to
  spacecraft
  629.47 TL793

ISBN 0-86272-373-6

Phototypeset by Southern Positives & Negatives
(SPAN), Lingfield, Surrey
Printed by Graficas Reunidas S.A. Madrid, Spain